From Bondage To
Breakthroughs

GALATIANS 5:1

Tamera Cotton

ISBN 978-1-64569-604-9 (paperback)
ISBN 978-1-64569-586-8 (hardcover)
ISBN 978-1-64569-587-5 (digital)

Christian Faith Publishing, Inc.
832 Park Avenue
Meadville, PA 16335
www.christianfaithpublishing.com

Printed in the United States of America

I want to dedicate this book to every one of God's chosen few. From the inmate to the ex-con, the hustler, prostitute, single mom, and the addict, this one's for you.

Contents

Preface

Whenever I tell someone about anything that I've done or if I tell them a story about one of my life experiences, the response is they can't believe it, like it's some sort of movie or something. I often get the reaction, "We don't look like what we been through," which is a blessing when it comes to me because I've been through so much. If I had to use one word for the purpose of me writing this book, it would be *relate*.

The devil often tries to convince us that we're the only person that has done something bad or hurtful. This way of thinking causes us to isolate from people or hide our wrongs instead of dealing with them. Utilizing the mercy of God is our help through it. Then feelings of shame or guilt set in. This is a playground for the enemy to do his work of prolonging our promise.

When we lack optimism, God cannot perform on the level he desires to perform on. In the words of one of my favorite pastor's, "The God you see is the God you get." Meaning, our vision of God needs to personify every name God goes by—from Jehovah Jireh to Strong Tower, to Immanuel, to the Good Shephard, Abba Father, Lion of Judah, the Messiah, just to name a few. We have to see God in every aspect of his deity.

I pray that through this book, your perspective of God's omnipresence is enlightened. Through me telling my story as unfiltered as possible, you may be able to relate to some aspect of it. Then utilizing it to assist you in the growth of your view of God's divine status.

This book is the epitome of me viewing God through eyes of vision. As I write this book, tears fall down my face when I look at my Christmas tree all decorated and lit up with no presents, none on the way and no means of income to provide them for my daughters. As you read this book, you'll get to know me and understand who I am. Tammy "The Hustler" being at peace with this is definitely the work of the Holy Spirit, my Comforter. Christmas is in eleven days and my heart is heavy, but I believe God, and I know everything happens for a reason. The experiences of my past and the situations of today, are all for the glory of the Lord. This and only this has brought me to a place where my bondage can become my breakthrough.

Introduction

If you belong to Christ, then you are Abraham's seed. And heirs according to the promise.

—Galatians 3:29

The scripture above does not come with any list of qualifications in order for you to belong to Christ. There are no hidden agendas or messy motives. One of the most beautiful things about God is that he qualifies those whom he calls. If God has called you to it, he will grow you through it. Throughout this book, you will read of some of my darkest seasons. However, you will notice the word of God that correlates to that particular time in my life although at that moment, I was unaware of God's presence and purpose.

This book is a reminder that God has been there all along. There is no situation where his presence was not present. As I looked back on my weak moments and fears, I became aware that God's grace and mercy was a very present help. God always seemed to be there in some way. It was not until I sat and wrote this book that I was enlightened on his ubiquitous glory.

> Where can I go from your spirit? Where can I flee from your presence? (Psalms 139:7, NIV)

This scripture is one of the first ones that literally spoke to me. During some of my darkest times, there was always some ray of hope. Now I know that was God all along strengthening me, allowing me to experience the side of him called Immanuel which means "God with us." Some situations can really make us feel like he is absent.

I remember being in prison, crying out to God. Then all of a sudden, an overwhelming enamor filled my cell. My comforter was there guiding me from despondency towards dependence on him. The Messiah wants to use our mistakes for his masterpiece. He can only do this for us if we spend time getting to know him. As you read further, I am definitely not a saint. However, by the grace of God, I am currently "saintified." In the past, the good news was proclaimed to me so many times I can't even count. It was of no value because I did not share the faith of those who obeyed. I chose to put my faith in fast money, lesbianism, prostitution, people, drugs, and much more. This lifestyle became my God, and I stayed in high pursuit.

When you've been where I've been and seen what I've seen, you'll subconsciously and gradually move into a state of learned helplessness. This is a condition in which a person suffers from a sense of powerlessness arising from traumatic events. Nevertheless, our God is so good.

> He gives strength to the weary and increases the power of the weak (Isaiah 40:29).

There is nothing you have ever experienced that God can't use for his glory. Your perceived setbacks were setups for God to show himself strong in that situation. This personally increases our faith in him and motivates us to tell someone just how good God is, proclaiming his goodness no matter how hard the test might seem. However, testimonies are void of value if you never pass the test. Remain a student in the classroom of Christ.

Chapter 1

History

But God chose the foolish things of the
world to shame the wise; God chose the weak
things of the world to shame the strong.
                            —1 Corinthians 1:27 (NIV)

I wanted to introduce myself as the female version of Paul, like a "Paulette" or something. Then I prayed about it; and God literally said, "No, love, you are doing too much." This is not the time for that. I love how he responds to me on my level. It's amazing to me. God is omniscient and still loves me enough to educate and correct me on my level. That's love.

My name is Tamera Cotton, and the world nicknamed me Tammy. While gangbanging in the housing projects of Chicago, they called me T-smoove. This name was the total opposite of me because I was one rough young lady at that time. Then when I sold drugs on the south side of Chicago, they called me Te-Te. Next is when I became a stripper. They called me Hypnotic. That name stuck the longest and became my Goliath, but we'll get more into that later on in the book. Looking back, I didn't realize how many names/mask that I actually wore.

Therefore, it was only right that when I became a praying and obeying child of God that a name change had to occur. I will now declare and decree that my new name is Testimony Tammy. Although the world gave me this name, Tammy, God knew I would be one of his living testimonies, representing his amazing grace and how everything is in his plan. When I say *everything*, I mean *everything*. Some people, places, and things that we think are irrelevant can play a key role in our process. Just the thought of God organizing my outcome brings hope to my heart. Glory be to God for having a plan even before I allowed the world to delay who God predestined me to be.

> For I know the plans I have for you, declares the Lord, plans to prosper you and not to harm you, plans to give you hope and a future. (Jeremiah 29:11, NIV)

I'm going to give you a brief background on who I am. As you read along, I pray that you see aspects of your story in mine. That way, together we'll know Immanuel (the God who is with us) orchestrated it all. If God is with us, then no weapon formed against us shall prosper.

I'm the oldest of four kids on my mother's side, and I don't know who I'm related to on my father's side. Born on the west side of Chicago but raised in the streets of "Chiraq" as the media likes to call it. Nevertheless, I like to call it "the real world." I believe Chicago has an anointing to challenge your character. If you consistently operate in integrity, then you should have no problem rising to the challenge, and you'll be safe in "the real world".

I remember as a child, we went to Church every week. I had to be around eight or nine years old. We had one of those old school preachers who would do a lot of coughing and heavy breathing during his sermon. I would often fall asleep during that time. That was one of the reasons why as a child, I was eager to do something in the church that would keep me awake after the praise and worship songs, trying to avoid those shocking secret pinches I'd get for falling asleep. I always loved to keep busy, and I still do to a certain extent. Now I just make sure it's business and not just busy-ness.

Nevertheless, back then, I was busy. First, I joined the choir which did not last too long. We could not afford the many robes and uniforms required for the different occasions. Then I became the youngest at the time to join The Usher Board. They had one uniform to wear every week. That was better on our budget, although I really didn't care what I wore. As long as I was able to do something in the church, I was happy. Looking back at things with a spiritual eye, I can see why the devil attacked me with a vengeance. I genuinely enjoyed serving the people of God, even as a youth.

Up until my early teenage years, I lived with my mother who was a single parent. After consistent behavior issues, I was then placed into foster care. I don't know my father. I could count on one hand how many times I encountered him. I've only heard stories about him and how some people say I'm just like him. Nevertheless, before I went into foster care, I remember moving to the housing projects. This is where my young life took a turn for the worst.

Living in the projects, I used to get jumped on after school almost every day. And let's not forget psychology says the oldest child is the so-called hero. I was far from heroic back then. There was this one project family that was obsessed with me. Literally the oldest brother used to punch me and fight me every chance he could get. The short ugly cousin would constantly pull my hair and pick fights with me. After a while, I was used to running home from school or leaving early, trying to avoid the inevitable.

I could not understand why they taunted me because we were so poor. Literally I remember wearing thin "white girl gym shoes" as we called them in the snow. Since I've grown in my relationship with God, I have learned that people saw a light in me. The devil tried his hardest to put out a glow that I never even knew was there. This glow is in you as well, even if you don't feel like it. People may see it clearly before you even realize it's there.

Therefore never be afraid of anyone, God is always in control.

> Be strong and courageous. Do not be afraid or terrified because of them, for the Lord your God goes with you; he will never leave you nor forsake you. (Deuteronomy 31:6, NIV)

After so many fights growing up in the projects, I learned that you needed a family of some sort just to survive. I decided to join a gang for protection, and it made me feel like someone had my back. I became a sister struggling with the sisters, as I like to call it. That's when I got the name T-smoove. I had to be about thirteen or fourteen years old back then. Once I did this, I didn't feel alone anymore. This was the first time I felt like I belonged to something. After moving so much, a desire to fit in and settle grew within me. This gang quenched that thirst for connection.

Nevertheless, I was fighting every day now, even jumping on girls, carrying around a bullet belt, just waiting for girls to say something disrespectful. I had my gang with me now, and I thought I was tough. I was even on the bone-crushing crew. That meant if a member was late for a meeting or did something corrupt, I was the one who gave out the mouth shots. Isn't it crazy how at first, I was the one running home; and then the moment, I had a team behind me? All of a sudden, I became Layla Ali. I never knew.

> The Lord will fight for you: you need to only be still. (Exodus14:14, NIV)

While in a gang, we wanted to make some money. We grew tired of fighting and being broke. We tried to get a building and sell drugs where we were from, but the guys were not allowing that. This is when I began my first hustle, stealing. We started off stealing stacks of thin shirts from expensive clothing stores where I would take them back and exchange it or get a check mailed to me. We started making money stealing from these stores all across Illinois. I started getting banned from stores all across Illinois.

Our thinking was so messed up. We thought it was actually a job, getting up early in the morning asking who's going to work today. It got so bad. I remember just driving to the front door, popping the trunk while my "friends" ran in with garbage bags and filled it up with clothes. Good Samaritan's would try to chase us, but we would fight or pepper spray them.

I was a greed-driven hot mess. This thirstiness began my lifestyle at the juvenile detention center. By this time, I was already a ward of the state, so I was in and out of foster care and in and out of juvenile detention. After numerous times in juvenile detention, they sent me away to Provo, Utah. This was a placement facility that was for teens with behavioral issues, so I fit the criteria perfectly. I was supposed to be closely monitored as I receive cognitive behavioral therapy. I still remember my therapist's name was Trish. She thought I needed love. I think she was right about that.

Nevertheless, to everyone's surprise, I came back home pregnant with my first daughter. I was fifteen years old, just a baby having a baby. Everyone thought this pregnancy was the best thing that could have ever happened to me, thinking this would definitely slow me down, and motherhood would be good for me.

Yet soon, as I had my oldest daughter, a friend who can't have kids fell in love with her. She babysat for me all the time, becoming so attached to my daughter. She began to think she was her mother. I did nothing to subdue the situation because I was outside every day. The greed seed the devil planted took root in my spirit so heavy now that I had my daughter. I believed I had to make money "by any means necessary" which is exactly what the devil wanted me to think. I had no idea that those seeds the devil was planting in my mind would have me taking forty years for an eleven-day journey.

Chapter 2

Group Homes

For who so ever does the will of my father in
heaven is my brother and sister and mother.
—Matthew 12:50 (NIV)

Briefly I told you about being in different group homes
and foster care. In addition, I want to explain my experiences in a few of these places. I can still remember my
first foster home. She made a living doing housekeeping at
upscale hotels in the downtown area, decorating her house
so beautifully, like something out of an interior design mag-
azine. If visiting the household, the beauty would blind
you to the brokenness that lies beneath the dissonance that
lingered under the surface.

The carnal eye would be amazed at how beautiful,
smart, hardworking, creative, and loving she was. However,
as I look back with the spiritual eye, I see right through
this façade. Looking down deep at a broken woman loaded
down with secret sins, portraying this sweet and help-
ful image to the counselors, her coworkers, and boy toys
meanwhile maintaining an unconcerned, cold, and distant
demeanor with these foster kids in her very own home, as if
we are some sort of shameful secret she wishes to keep hid-

den, only showcasing us orphans when the compensation was in jeopardy.

> For God will bring every deed into judgment, including every hidden thing, whether it is good or evil. (Ecclesiastes 12:14, NIV)

She would secretly beat us with extension cords, belts, shoes, pots, and pans, anything she could get her hands on, chasing us around the house as we ran for our lives, making us lie on the floor naked and get beatings until she was tired. We had to have the house in immaculate condition by the time she arrived from work, the kitchen cleaned, floor mopped and trash taken out.

Nevertheless, if I washed the dishes and hadn't put them away before she walked in, I was getting my head banged into the cabinets until the last dish was put away. Consequently in front of counselors, the bruises became accidents. Mommy Dearest is what the orphans called her. She never wanted to appear as if she didn't have it all together.

> Charm is deceptive, and beauty is fleeting: but a woman who fears the Lord, is to be praised. (Proverbs 31:30, NIV)

Furthermore, my counselor moved me from this foster home. I was placed in another foster home which appeared to be better at first. I was about thirteen years old. This lady had three boys and a girl there already. The girl was her biological daughter, so she was a bit favored. Her daughter and I became very close. We were only a year apart in age.

We would share clothes, talk all night and even sneak outside together. I thought she was my best friend. I genuinely started to love her like the real sister I never had.

Deceived by all her acts of kindness, thinking it came from a place of love because she had the ability and resources, while in freshman year together, I became very social, and she began to despise me. In contrast, when I was not around, she would gossip about me like the filth she really thought I was, exploiting the secrets I shared with her for her own personal glory or gossip. Our mutual friend would tell me. I just never wanted to believe it.

> All of us have become like one who is unclean, an all our righteous acts are like filthy rags; we all shrivel up like a leaf, and like the wind our sins sweep us away. (Isaiah 64:6, NIV)

The three boys in the house all had a different spirit of perversion. The baby boy was the black sheep of the family, staying in and out of trouble. I remember telling her that he rubbed his private with mine every time we were alone and that I was scared to be alone with him. I recall being afraid when everyone had to leave the house. It was so casual to him that he did it to me every time he saw me.

Then my foster mom's husband was a taxi driver part-time. He would normally be the one picking us up from school, church, or activities. This guy was nasty. He would pull his private out when he picked us up and be playing with his self while driving a van full of kids. We told her, but she would discreetly ignore it, not willing to jeopardize her sponsor/husband for us. You would have never known this level of perversion was going on in such a beautiful house.

> As they were increased, so they sinned against me: therefore will I change their glory into shame. (Hosea 4:7, KJV)

I can't forget a new foster girl came into the house, and the baby brother started to do the same, grinding thing to her that he had been doing to me. This new girl was not having it though. She said it was not right, and she was going to tell. That was the last I seen of her. She was quietly and quickly removed. This really made me stay quiet. I had nowhere else to go. I had been running through group homes and foster homes left and right. My counselor appeared to be tired of finding me new living situations.

I started to think that all these homes washed things under the table, that these places all had some sort of secret evil. Eventually I was removed; yet when I left this house, I thought about her real daughter was the only girl left in a house of horny men. Looking back, it was extremely odd that she would still be sleeping in the bed with her grown brother. Nonetheless, she would never admit something like that happened to her. She hated me when I finally told the truth and revealed it was happening to me. I believe she was conditioned to keep quiet.

> Then you will know the truth, the truth shall set you free. (John 8:32, NIV)

After being in these different foster homes and being physically abused and sexually abused, you would think my counselor would stop it with the foster homes by now. Nevertheless, she placed me in another one. This woman was a preacher and had foster kids. This was the foster home I stayed at the longest. She made everyone go to church every Sunday, and she would have Bible classes in the house on Wednesday and prayer on Saturdays. I was in church, church, and more church.

Besides me, there were three girls that were real sisters she had been raising since they were little. They would stick together like glue which can be a good thing and a bad thing. If the mother showed me any attention, I became an outcast to the sisters.

Our foster mother was very driven to build a church. She's had a church at the house, and she rented locations. Yet her congregation never grew. It was always just me and the girls. Friends would come to visit sometimes, but no one ever joined for many years. She never gave up trying to build a church congregation. I can't remember a time when she was not reading the Word. We would joke and say eventually she is going to start reading the maps. She even gained degrees and awards in theology. People paid her to preach the Word of God.

Consequently with the same tongue, she would curse you out like a sailor, hold a grudge for abnormal amounts of time, and gossip for hours on the phone about us foster kids. It was mentally overwhelming. One minute, I felt loved. Then the next minute, I was walking on eggshells, hoping not to make the wrong move. I was scared to come out of my room not knowing which personality I was dealing with that day.

Then our pastor/foster mother started to get sick, often having a number of strokes. It was sad to watch her having the strokes and the sisters' reaction to it. They appeared as if they could not live without her. Looking back, it was less like a family and more like a cult. The crazy part is when we visited her in the hospital the last time before the counselor removed us, she said she realized that God gave her these strokes for the people around her which is shocking that she would even think this way. I watched this lady read the Bible day and night, praying for countless hours. For her to say that God allowed this sickness on her body for the people around her and not for her own revelation was baffling to me even then. Nevertheless, I have learned there is a big difference in studying the Word and rightly dividing it. Then it's a whole other thing to obey what it says.

> Ever learning, and never able to come to the knowledge of the truth. (2 Timothy 3:7, KJV)

The stroke consists of every time she sat up to move around, she had a slurred speech. Basically every time she tried to walk, she could not talk. Every time you try to walk, you cannot talk. Every time you tried to walk, you cannot talk.

Now I am not a reverend, preacher, elder, teacher, doctor, evangelist, apostle, or anything else, just a humble student of the Word of God. Nevertheless, I thank God for wisdom. If my stroke consists of "every time I tried to walk, I cannot talk, and I am a preacher," wisdom tells me that my walk must not be lining up with what I'm talking about.

> But be ye doers of the word, and not hearers only, deceiving your own selves (James 1:22, KJV).

Chapter 3

My Testimony

> The rich think their wealth protects them.
> They imagine themselves safe behind it.
> —Proverbs 18:11 (MSG)

Once I was old enough to pack my bags and leave those group homes, I signed a lease for my first apartment on the south side of Chicago in the Englewood area. Now this building looked worse than the projects. It had guys shooting dice in one entrance and selling drugs in the other one. My friend Rosa, whom I knew from the projects, connected me with the landlord. She said, "As long as I have the cash, he has keys." Rosa was a little older than all the rest of our little crew. She was a cool light-skinned chick who was very short, almost midget height. She also had a lot of kids, so many I can't remember exactly. One thing I do remember is she knew how to throw some parties. Everyone would show up for Rosa's parties. She had these loudspeakers. You could hear the music a block away.

I moved into the other entrance from her. I was so excited for my first apartment. I didn't care that the floor was lopsided, and the furniture came with roaches in it. I felt like I was independent and that felt great. In my mind, I was making power moves for real. Now, Rosa would throw parties all the time. I didn't know anyone in the neighborhood but her, so I went to the majority of them. Rosa loved to have a good time, and she loved men even more.

One day, I came over, and her new boy toy was there with his brother. The brother looked good like Trey Songz in a suit, very clean cut, handsome, professional with slacks and loafers on. For some odd reason, he just didn't belong over Rosa's house. She wanted to hook us up together so bad. He was in high pursuit of me as well.

I can't lie. I was wooed by his eloquence of words. Being from the housing projects, this type of man was different for me. Then he had the nerve to be down to earth and partying with us. I partied with him all night and took him back to my place the first night. As I think back on our first sexual encounter, something was not right. Of course, I couldn't put my finger on it. He was very vulgar, rude, and extremely aggressive. Yet when it was over, he was back so nice and romantic which made me overlook it and not read too much into his behavior during our first sexual encounter.

Eventually we started dating heavy. He gave me money and bought me expensive gifts. I remember him popping up with this powder pink peacoat and some powder pink alligator cowboy boots. At this time, I was like about nineteen years old, so cowboy boots definitely were not on my shopping list. He was in his late thirties, so this was his style. I'll admit I was feeling him and his constant thoughtfulness. His charisma made me accept the old-lady gifts he bought me with excitement.

One day, he showed up unannounced saying, "Let's go for a ride." I hopped in carelessly. He took me to his storage facility downtown. As he went in, I waited in the car. He came out with the biggest bag of drugs I had ever seen in my life. I rode around with him as he dropped it off to different people. Meanwhile, as we were riding, he started to tell me how he had a good product, that it was better than the guys in my building. If I just sold a little something out my back door for him, we were about to make a lot of money.

This man's words were so enticing as if nothing could go wrong. Of course, you know I did it. And it seems like instantly, the man came with people to put gates on my front and back door. I learned how to cook, weigh, and bag up drugs very quick. He even had different guys coming over to sit with me as security while other guys were outside sending drug addicts to purchase it. I mean this man must have planned this. In less than a week, we were in full drug business. My back door was officially the crack house for dealers and users.

Once the money started rolling in, I never really saw him, only to drop off drugs and to pick up money. He'd tell me he was working on the outside of things. After a couple of months, I was making more money than I had ever seen before. I did a lot of shopping but never went anywhere to wear anything I bought. I was always in the house, selling drugs out the back door.

Unexpectedly one day, Rosa called and said all of our friends from the projects came out here to party with us. I got dressed and went over Rosa's house for a little while. We hung out briefly, but they wanted me to go back to the projects with them. I figured my man wouldn't mind because I hadn't been outside since we started this hustle. I partied the night away and didn't get back until around 1:00 a.m. My friends did not want the night to end, so they came back with me.

As we walked into Rosa's house, he was playing cards with a wifebeater on like he's been there all night. He smiled and hopped up to hug me and said, "What's up, baby? Where you been?" I was a little intoxicated but still alert and excited to see him.

My response was "nowhere, baby I went to the projects for a while to visit."

He responded calmly, "Like that's cool, baby," then pulled me close, kissed my forehead, and whispered in my ear, "Let's talk in the bathroom." I didn't think anything of the whisper because the music is always so loud at Rosa's house. The lights were dim as well. so he had to pull me close.

Once he locked that bathroom door, he instantly turned into someone I never saw before. He began to choke me, saying I need to ask permission to go outside and that I made him miss a lot of money. He began fighting me so badly that his punch blacked both my eyes and almost broke my nose.

I was so scared and shocked I didn't know what to do. It all happened so fast. He told me to hurry up and get myself together and go straight out the front door quick. I did exactly what he said. With the music playing loud and the lights so dim, no one even noticed.

He followed me back to my apartment. I didn't want to let him in. Nevertheless, he was very strong and forced his way, not only in my apartment but in my body as well. He raped me that night. I can't tell you if I said no or if the shock of it all silenced me, but I know for a fact that I did not want it. The man was chocking me with a vengeance, holding me down, and shoving his private inside of me extremely rough. It hurt so bad I remember punching and pushing him with tears filling my eyes. Then I remember in the midst of it all, I just gave up and let him finish. It was like I went into some sort of trance or something. Seriously!

This man got up off me and went into the bathroom like nothing ever happened. I heard the water running in the bathroom, so I figured he was washing up. He was still talking to me, but I have no idea what he was saying. I couldn't move. It was like I was frozen in time. My mind was blank, and my body stayed still. My eyes filled with tears that would not come out.

Once the front door slammed, my whole body jumped, and I felt cold. Immediately I went to the bathroom. It was like I was in some sort of outer-body experience at that moment, moving in slow motion. For instance, I slowly sat on the toilet, unrolled some tissue, and wiped myself. Once I saw the blood, reality set in, and tears streamed down my face. My vagina began to hurt, as well as my heart. I realized I had just been raped by my own boyfriend.

As I type this part of my testimony, it brings tears to my eyes all over again, nevertheless for a different reason because although I went through that experience, I did not remember much detail until now that God has me writing this book. I now believe God was my comforter, putting me in that trance-like state. I am even more amazed at God's grace and love. The Word of God says,

> But the Comforter, which is the Holy Ghost, whom the Father will send in my name, he shall teach you all things, and bring all things to your remembrance, whatsoever I have said unto you. (John 14:26, KJV)

Immediately I left him alone. He called and popped up at my house for a while, but I couldn't stand to see the man. It never crossed my mind that I should have called the police or told somebody. He acted so normally about it that I was confused, thinking like, *Does this man actually realize what he did to my body?* Acting nonchalant about it like it was not a big deal, I just hid until he stopped calling and popping up.

Eventually, he stopped, but what didn't stop was the knocks at my back door. At first, I would ignore it until some of the guys told me that they knew other guys with a good product. We could still sell drugs ourselves. We didn't need him. I was down for it; and before I knew it, the suppliers were giving me stuff up front because I was moving it so fast. Now I'm deep into my second hustle, selling drugs for myself now.

After a few months passed, I heard he was in jail. I didn't celebrate that fast because right after that, Rosa died of AIDS, and I was heartbroken. I knew she had a lot of boyfriends, but I would never have thought AIDS would end her life. The building was not the same anymore with

Rosa gone. The only thing that kept me there was the greed seed I allowed the devil to water in my spirit.

Soon after that, my old counselor contacted me, saying someone from her church needed an office secretary. She thought I'd be perfect for the job since I used to work in that furniture-store office, answering phones and stuff. Little did she know, I was taking people's lay-away deposits, delivering furniture to my friends, and making them pay me for it. She had no idea all the little side hustles I did, and I was not about to tell her. The devil had a tight grip on my integrity and was not letting go.

APT Management hired me on the spot because of my ex-counselor's recommendation. My bosses were a humble Christian couple who were prosperous in business. The job was right down the street from my current apartment. I could leave the office and go straight to selling my drugs after. My new boss had a few buildings on the south side and a lot on the north side. He needed me to be in the south-side office. That way, he could attend to his main business on the north side. All I had to do was make sure the maintenance team fixed any issues in the tenant apartments. Come to the office and answer the calls, collect rent, and accept tenant complaints.

In return, I was getting a free apartment and cash every couple of weeks. This would have been a great way to start over, a free apartment and money. Nevertheless, I was in full blossom of that greed seed by now. The apartment was very nice, dark hardwood floors and spacious rooms. The inside and the outside of the building was very well-maintained. This was an amazing opportunity for a young girl like myself. At first, I never really moved in because when I got off work, I'd go hustle at my old apartment. I become so accustomed to hustling. I was blind to the value of this new opportunity right in front of me.

> Therefore, as we have opportunity, let us do good to all people, especially to those who belong to the family of believers. (Galatians 6:10, NIV)

My thoughts were, *I have to make this money while I still can.* I'd often be hustling in my old apartment by myself all night. Barely sleeping, the drugs were selling so fast, never realizing it was fertile ground for the devil to plant a few seeds. I started secretly calling the lesbian chat lines. Nothing major ever happened at first until I began to call all the time while I waited on customers to come to the back door.

One day, this guy happened to be on the lesbian side. We chatted for a while and came to find out he was downstairs in my building. Instantly we began a sexual relationship. Although his baby's mother lived right downstairs, he would still sneak upstairs to my apartment when she was at work. He got so comfortable that he would even serve some of the customers at the back door.

Eventually, she found out and wanted to fight me every chance she got. One night, I was sleeping in the bed; and the way my apartment was set up, I could lean out my bed and view the hallway. Something just happened to wake me up out my sleep. (I know now that it was God.) I got up to investigate the front door. It was a pile of dust, as if someone tried to chisel his or her way around the wood panel of the lock. Immediately I called him to come and get me and drop me off at the new apartment. I never slept over there before, but something was telling me it's time to go. I packed up all the drugs and money, grabbed a bag of clothes, and left.

When I came back in the morning, the apartment was completely broken into. I knew it was the work of his baby's mother because they poured bleach on my clothes and in my television. If it was drug-related, they would have stolen the television. Only God knows who was with her and what they had planned to do to me. I'm so thankful that God makes a way of escape even when we don't realize the danger we are in.

> There hath no temptation taken you but such as is common to man: but God is faithful, who will not suffer you to be tempted above that ye are able; but will with the temptation also make a way of escape, that ye may be able to bear it. (1 Corinthians 10:13, KJV)

I should have left her baby's father there with her, yet I moved him with me. There was never a dull moment once this man entered my life. He came on a mission straight from Satan himself. This man was physically and mentally abusive to me. I remember one time, he beat me up so badly in front of my oldest daughter. My nose began to bleed uncontrollably and I had to go to the hospital. He would be waiting in my apartment with shotguns, just sitting in the dark. We had a very dangerous love affair. If we were not having sex, we were abusing each other. I got pregnant by this man three times, and I aborted them all. Being involved with him was like a dark cloud followed me. I was constantly in and out of jail, catching drug cases or domestics. You name it. I was charged with it.

That forced me to take a break on the drug dealing. I tried to just work the little office job my ex-counselor had got me. Instead that seed of greed the devil had planted kept telling me, "That was not enough money." I need to come up with something and quick. I let the devil convince me to make a hustle out of my opportunity.

Now my boss at the management company was blessed abundantly with his buildings all over. He also had other business ventures and a beautiful family. All he really wanted to do was drive by the south side office, pick up the rent, and keep it moving. I made sure he got his rent money every month from "his" tenants.

Although I began to have the maintenance workers fix some of the entrances that my boss knew was closed for repairs, I started moving people in as if it was my building. Having them pay rent and security deposits to me. I paid the maintenance men to fix the apartments and to keep quiet about what I was doing. I was absent of integrity then, and I still feel bad about it now.

One of my friends didn't want to pay any more. She called my boss and told him everything. They gave me the steel-toe boot, and I deserved it. I apologized to them, and they accepted it. But I still want to take this opportunity to publicly apologize to them again. (I am truly sorry.) My ex-counselor, on the other hand, never forgave me. I wrote her letters and slipped her notes. I can't blame her though.

I took her name and brought it to a disgrace. She stuck her neck out for me, and this is what I did. I'm truly sorry from the bottom of my heart.

> Jesus said "Father, forgive them, for they know not what they are doing." And they divided up his clothes by casting lots. (Luke 23:34, NIV)

Chapter 4

Friends

One who has unreliable friends soon comes to ruin,
but there is a friend who sticks closer than a brother.
—Proverbs 18:24 (NIV)

I used to have this best friend. Her name was Toya. She was extremely pretty, with a petite frame, and very down to earth. Toya would help me sell my drugs even though she didn't have to. She was very spoiled which made her a little eager to do something with her time. Me on the other hand, I had to hustle hard just to barely make ends meet, always trying to come up with some new hustle or scam which can be exciting for my "friends" but exhausting for myself.

Anyway I used to hustle drugs for her stepdad. He was the man in our neighborhood back then. One day, I came over Toya's house. She had a new girl over I had never seen before. Yet they were getting dressed to go party with some guy. I didn't think much of it because Toya was always meeting random girls and befriending them. At that time, I was not a party girl, so I just organized my drugs so I could go hustle. Then I left.

The following day, Toya had a story to tell me, come to find out this was not your average party. It was a stripper party, and the guy was some sort of pimp. She was not down with being pimped, but the stripper lifestyle was enticing to her. Toya didn't start dancing right off the back. She wanted me to go with her to a few parties just to check out the scene, convincing me that it was money involved.

When I first got there, I did not like it at all. This place was a "hole in the wall" club for real. Upstairs is where the bar, DJ, and the dance floor was located. The stripper's did floor shows and lap dances. Meanwhile, the pimps watched and collected. It was like something straight out of *The Players Club*. Then in the basement was the dressing room and where the supposedly VIP section was located. I remember once I watched this pimp choke this girl to sleep down there. Nobody said or did anything, even the guys just watched.

This so-called VIP was where guys would pay a little extra cash to go into this leaky basement with sheets sectioning off different areas. Then the girl of their choice could do something strange for a "little change." The thought of me having my clothes off in front of them repulsed me. The type of guys that were there looked like guys I was hustling my drugs with in the streets. Nevertheless, in Toya's mind, this was about to become her second home. Little did I know, it was about to be mine as well.

However, in the beginning, I just watched as the devil watered that greed seed that grew inside my spirit. After a few times of watching the strippers make money, I was telling Toya, "Let's go buy me some stripper clothes." Now the first few times I went, I was so uncomfortable and nervous. I just stayed at the bar, talking and drinking. Toya, on the other hand, was an instant professional. She was socializing through the club like she been there for years. I was so pathetic. She would feel sorry for me and just give me money for coming with her. I really loved my friend, and I felt as if we both had each other backs. She was always there for me.

> Two are better than one because they have a good return for their labor: If either of them falls down, one can help the other up. But pity anyone who falls and has no one to help them up. (Ecclesiastes 4:9–10, KJV)

Although I was a terrible stripper, we became regulars at this club. You would rarely see white men come inside. Therefore, when you did see one, it was like the green light came on, and sirens went off in the dressing room. The strippers and the pimps were on his heels quick. After a while, I realized the more drinks I had, the more relaxed and talkative I became. In turn, I was more sociable and made more money. Eventually, it took a minimum of one blunt and two drinks just for me to even come out of the dressing room. In order to make the money, I had to be under the influence.

> Likewise, teach the older women to be reverent in the way they live, not to be slanderers or addicted to much wine, but to teach what is good. (Titus 2:3, NIV)

Now after a while, I started hanging out with other strippers. The new strippers exposed me to different stripper parties every night. I became friends with this one dancer named Strawberry. She was really cool. She also worked at a coffee shop downtown. Strawberry always kept some sort of money-making scheme going on. Her hustle game was nonstop, which was right up my alley. Eventually she got me hired at the coffee house also. We'd be selling coffee in the morning and our bodies at night. What a way to spend our day.

Strawberry also introduced me to this new internet website she heard through the grapevine. We could create an account. Then we could sell our bodies for money. We would post pictures of ourselves and phone number online, then wait for men to call us. They would pay extreme amounts for sex, and sometimes there would be no sex involved.

At first, we didn't really post that often because we were more into the stripper-party scene. It became a lifestyle for me more than it was an income. Every single night, I went out to make money. I recall one day, my youngest daughter was about six years old. She was like "Ma-Ma, why didn't you get all the money last night? You have to go every night." Hearing that broke my heart that night. Although it was not enough to make me stay in the house and out the streets, my little girl never seems to amaze me. I believe God speaks right through her. I often tell her she's my miracle baby.

> Children are a heritage from the Lord, offspring a reward from him. (Psalms 127:3, NIV)

My daughters are gifts from God himself, and I love them both abundantly. I pray right now that my oldest daughter reads this book; and through my testimony, she believes in God. She's headed down a dangerous path right now, one that I am all too familiar with and stayed way too long. Yet if God can change me, I believe he can change anybody. I stay in constant prayer for her to realize who God is and to make better decisions for her future, also for her to understand the call on her life that she must answer!

> But small is the gate and narrow the road that leads to life, and only a few find it. (Matthew 7:14)

Now after being in the strip-club life for a while, it seemed like me and Toya grew further and further apart. Then I met this Mexican girl and started to hang out with her. Instantly we started to hustle together every day. She was just as thirsty as I was, if not more. I even introduced her to the internet hustle, but we liked the streets more at first.

After a few months of hustling the strip clubs together, she got pregnant. She had an abusive boyfriend/pimp and now the baby's father. Once she became pregnant, he put an urgency in her for making money, much so that one day, she came to my house with this new phone, wanting me to post her online and drive her around, and she would pay me. She wanted me to keep the phone so her boyfriend would think she was just dancing. I didn't really care. I was like "Okay, let's do it."

> For the lips of the adulterous woman drip honey, and her speech is smoother than oil. (Proverbs 5:3, NIV)

This was how the floodgates really opened. It was like she was a natural. Out of all my hustles, this one became the most profitable. We started to do it every single day. I stopped dancing instantly. Every now and then, we would pop in and out of the strip club just to recruit a few new girls. Word spreads fast, and girls started to come from everywhere. Once I didn't want to go to the south side to pick up some girl, her mom dropped her off to me. It was crazy now that I'm looking back on it. I used to keep a different group of girls at my house all the time. Then I'd have another group at the hotels downtown. It was times I had two cars and still had to rent one because I had girls in hotels all over Chicago.

It was a lot of money, and it was a lot of headaches. I felt like I was under so much pressure. This pressure was so overwhelming. I started taking ecstasy really heavy. I felt as if I was obligated to make something happen for them while they were around, whether it was a trick, bachelor party, or stripper party. At the end of the day, I was pimping them, and they were pimping me as well.

> Better is little with fear of the Lord than great wealth and turmoil. (Proverbs 15:16, NIV)

Now by this time, Toya heard what I was doing, and she started her own little team of girls. With her being spoiled already, it was not about the money. It was more so about partying and competing with me. She also had become a lesbian after a while.

Her new girlfriend definitely affected her thoughts toward me, convincing her that we were in some sort of competition, sealing the deal to the end of our friendship. Her girlfriend realized how lucrative Toya's girls were and wanted to isolate her.

> A false witness shall not be unpunished, and he that speaketh lies shall not escape. (Proverbs 19:5, KJV)

One day, my girls and I pulled up side by side with Toya and her girls to the local strip club. Now one of the girls did not lock my car door, and I left my laptop and a giant designer bag of dance clothes in the car. Once we were inside the party, I was drinking and smoking heavily. I believe I saw Toya's girlfriend leave out and come back in. This could have been the drugs and liquor playing on my hate for Toya's girlfriend.

Nevertheless, once we got home, my laptop was missing, and this was my money maker. I was furious and convinced Toya's girlfriend did it. The next morning, we went over to her house. I intended on just taking my laptop, yet things did not go quite as planned. The Mexican girl and I had planned to go upstairs while the other girls stayed in the car. I planned to beat up Toya's girlfriend if she decided to say anything. I believe now I just wanted to fight her girlfriend for fueling the separation between me and my friend. I had anger with my friend also for believing her new lover over her old friend.

In conclusion, once I reached the top of the stairs, I started to scream and go crazy on her girlfriend. She would not put Toya's daughter down. I could smell the fear on her that day. Finally, she went to the back to lay the baby down, then came to the front. We started to go at it like two wild beasts. In the meantime, the Mexican girl was unplugging the laptop. Toya ran to the front and jumped into the fight. Now I'm fighting them both.

I reached in my back pocket and pulled out my box cutter. As soon as my arm swung upwards, The box cutter opened and sliced Toya across the face. It all just happened so fast I couldn't believe it. The moment seemed as if time stood still, shocked in a state of disbelief. All the fighting stopped, and we were all froze as the blood dripped from her face. I still can't believe I sliced my best friend in her face when I really just wanted to say I missed her. Many times I apologized, wrote letters, and sent messages, but she can never forgive me. I don't blame her.

> A brother offended is harder to be won than a strong city: and their contentions are like the bars of a castle. (Proverbs 18:19, KJV)

Chapter 5

Miracles

> Immediately the boy's father exclaimed, "I do
> believe; help me overcome my unbelief!"
> —Mark 9:24 (NIV)

I started dating my second girlfriend after one of my many incarcerations. Now I know I haven't told you about the first girlfriend yet. I'll enlighten you on that devil later. Nevertheless, my second girlfriend was a much older woman, who was very professional. She worked as a gossip blogger, so I believe that's where she gained her long-winded conversations from.

This woman played more mind games than the cops on *Criminal Minds*. She would go to sleep nagging and wake up nagging. It was exhausting just being around her. She would talk for abnormal amounts of time, long dramatic lectures that never ended with a resolution, using big words that I believed she would Google before we argued.

> Sin is not ended by multiplying words, but the prudent hold their tongues. (Proverbs 10:19, NIV)

I could never delight myself in long-winded people, thinking they were trying to convince me of something not true or sell me something I did not need. That's one of the main reasons I am shocked that God has me writing this book. Long conversations are not my style at all. I like straight-to-the-point people. Yet as I write and God brings things to my remembrance, it seems like my whole life has been long-winded.

Consequently, she just talked way too much and enjoyed instigating. We would get into arguments and fights so much it became normal for us. On one particular night, our arguing lead to fighting. I just came in from a party about 2:00 a.m., so I was very drunk which in her sober mind meant it is time to deal with our issues. Mixing fighting with liquor was a recipe for disaster with me. Before I knew it, she was bleeding. I just cut her arm.

To me, it was a little baby cut. But to her, she cried like a baby, putting on this sympathy show that was worth an academy award, hugging me and professing her love and how this was her fault too which is exactly what I wanted to hear to finally end this night, basically just trying to make up to appear as if it's over. Nevertheless, she had other plans because soon as we went to bed together, a couple of hours later, I woke up to the police with guns out, and she was hiding behind them.

They stated that she called a while ago and said I assaulted her which means this girl slithered out of the bed while I was sleeping, then vindictively hid somewhere to go call the police. In anticipation of seeing me behind bars, I went straight to jail. She knew I was already out on bond for cutting my best friend. Then I have the audacity to catch another stabbing case with my background. My file was full of domestics by this time—from my baby daddy, street fights, and now lesbian fights. When I went to court, I instantly had no bond, so there is no escaping the end results.

Both my cases where at the domestic court building. Ironically, I had court on the same day. It just happened to be in different court rooms. I couldn't believe it. I was in the holding cell worried to death, pacing back and forth, girls looking at me like I was a nut case. I chatted with my lawyer a second. Next, they put me in a private cell closer to my courtroom. My lawyer really didn't bring me any good news, giving me the routine lawyer lingo.

Once I got alone in the cell, it seemed like an eternity before they called me. I recall thinking to myself like, *I am about to do some serious time.* There is no way outta this one with two stabbings in the same building on the same day. Also with my violent background, I'm convinced I am about to sit this one out. Worried and in a state of panic, I thought I needed to pray. I got on my knees back there and cried out to God Almighty for help.

> In my distress I called upon the Lord, and cried unto my God: he heard my voice out of the temple, and my cry came before him, even into his ears. (Psalms 18:6, KJV)

Soon as I got off my knees, the officer was calling my name. He unlocked the gate as I wiped the tears from my eyes. I went in front of the judge for the case against my ex-best friend first. When I walked out, I didn't see her. Usually she'll be right in front of the judge with the lawyers between us. However, recently we have been having mix-ups with the court dates and switched locations. *So she probably was running late*, I thought.

The judge looked at my face with a firm tone and said to the state, "Where is the victim?" Before the state could complete her response, the judge stated she was tired of this back and forth, constantly continuing my case with no victim, "Case dismissed." I was in a total shock. She never even opened my file. The mix-up was God mixing up a miracle. Glory be to God!

After a while, they escorted me to my next court room on another floor.

This judge was tough. I previously had him for another domestic earlier this year. He knew my face and was sick of seeing it. Now when I walked into the courtroom, I saw my ex-girlfriend. She had her arm around her new girlfriend or whoever the girl was. That was one of the old-lady mental games she liked to play.

The judge was like "nice to see you again, Ms. Cotton." I smiled and was like "hello, Judge," Thinking in the back of my mind like, *Something is not right with him today.* He started off reciting my rap sheet. It was like a never-ending story. I felt smaller and smaller with every word that came out of the judge's mouth. Some of my charges I forgot I even did. As I faced the judge, I could feel my ex- girlfriend's eyes burning a hole in the back of my neck.

The state even chimed in with his two cents that nobody requested. Once my rap sheet recital was over. The judge said, "My rap sheet speaks for itself. I need some kind of help. Obviously incarceration is not working. I'm mandating you to counseling." In a compassionate tone, he also stated, "Your free to go, Ms. Cotton. Don't let me down." My soul leaped for joy. I couldn't help but crack a smile, especially when I looked back and saw my ex-girl-friend storm out the court room in disappointment.

> Therefore they sought again to take him: but he escaped out of their hand. (John 10:39, KJV)

Behind the county-jail walls and the prison walls, I witnessed countless miracles like that, not only for myself but for roommates and even women on my tier I never met. I watched women cry out to God. Then immediately some new law gets passed and releases them all. I watched women try to take their own life, and God gave them their freedom. At the same time, I watched women take their own life, and I prayed that their soul went to heaven.

I remember once I was in the "hole" where all you hear is voices. People talk through the wall because you are all locked down. This is like a jail inside the jail, also called 23 and 1. Which means you are locked in a cell twenty-three hours a day and your allowed one hour out for calls and showers. In this area, you hope for and are lucky if you get a roommate. Just to have someone to talk to face-to-face. Sometimes, being alone with your thoughts can be good. And other times, it can be bad.

One night, while I was in the hole, a girl started singing church songs through her hole in the door, then another and another. Then before I knew it, the whole tier was taking turns singing church songs. It was so soothing that night. I slept peaceful in my cell.

> Sing praises to God, sing praises; sing praises to our King sing praises. (Psalm 47:6, NIV)

The very next morning, to my surprise, officers decided to clear out all inmates in the hole. They put everyone back into general population which subsequently never happened. It was definitely a miracle.

Looking back on it now, I'm in a state of amazement because I'd sweep my miracles right under the table like "oh yes, thank you, Lord," then back to doing what I want, minimizing the fact that it was a power greater than myself that just made that happen.

Glory be to God on December 23, 2015.

God has me in a total state of amazement right now! He has made a way out of no way. I am aware that this was a miracle and nothing short of it. As I began writing this book, God made me stop prostituting online. I'm responding to God like "Okay, I still have a part-time job and the African who I been with for years. He buys cars and pays all my bills so I can be content." Then almost immediately, I lost my job, and it's been real tight. Then I had to break open the piggy bank (literally).

I was heated on the inside because it is very close to Christmas. I don't have anything for my kids. Nothing! As I'm getting ready to go meet the African and give him my list, I prayed to God that I keep my peace. How many of us know that we better be careful with them prayers. Well, I was a newbie in prayer then, and God had a lesson in store.

The African loves to say I'm crazy when he tarries with my time, and I react in an uproar. Consequently he uses my reaction to give me the bare minimum. When we sat down for breakfast, I started small talk as I usually do, telling him how my friend came over, talking about her boyfriend wanting to marry her. I told her to tell him, "The proof is in the purchase." The next morning, she calls me and says she repeated to him, "The proof is in the purchase." Then while she was sleeping, the man went through her phone. He found out she had been prostituting online.

Then at that very moment, God said right through me, "I am too." This man couldn't believe what I just said and neither could I. I was so shocked I just told the man that has been helping with all my bills for the last three years that I am a prostitute, the man that I am prepared to give my list of Christmas demands to. Yet I repeated myself so calmly, saying, "Yes, I been prostituting the whole time we been together." This man was shocked. His eyes started to water, and he got up from the table and went to the bathroom.

Meanwhile, reality sat in on me like, "Really, God, the African has to go to huh?" As the words left my lips, it's like I was realizing exactly why God said I had to be done with him also. For years, I have been using men for money. When he came back from the bathroom, it's like I was not even in control of my lips anymore. I started telling this man all kinds of thing like "you want to keep me dependent on you." And He knows he gives me just enough money to keep me coming back, that in reality, I've been prostituting with him as well, just in a discreet way.

As I'm telling this man these things with my lips, it's like at the same time God was telling me with my lips. I know this sounds crazy but imagine how I felt doing it. It's not like I just leaped out on faith. I was definitely early in my walk with God. That's why I know God did that for real. I could not even imagine leaving who I thought was my main source of income right before Christmas. I just went with it, telling him it's over, and we need to part ways immediately.

He couldn't stomach the thought of his investment actually leaving him alone. He was willing to do anything, trying to keep me under his wing. Yet things were never the same. God had exposed me to a part of him that I never knew and a part of myself I never knew. And once a person is exposed, you become accountable to be fruitful.

Now I'm new at this completely sold-out "faithing it" thing, especially being so close to Christmas, with kids, no income and now no financial support. All I knew was I wanted to say yes to God, and I had no idea what was next. Consequently, I decided to take things into my own hands unaware that if God had brought me to it that he would bring me through it.

I went to my school and took out a loan, thinking I have to make something happen for my kids' Christmas. I know I hear the church folks say, "Faith without works is died." I decided to help God out a little bit. That way, I did my works. I even planned to sell all my flat screen TVs, thinking to myself like, *I can't turn back now.* Although when God steps in, he already has a plan.

> Be still and know that I am God: I will be exalted among the heathen, I will be exalted in the earth (Psalms 46:10, KJV).

The loan still hasn't come, and I never had to touch my TVs. Out of the clear blue sky, my friends brother called me saying, "Do I remember doing his taxes last year?"

I said, "Yes, I still have your card."

"Great, because the IRS say they released my funds on the 16th." I checked that card so quick. And yes, his tax money was on there.

He paid me in full and gave me a blessing. He never knew God had used him to show me a miracle. Never again will I minimize my miracles. I am completely aware that God made that way for Christmas 2015.

As I type this part of the book on Christmas Eve and our tree is filled with gifts, I am fully persuaded we serve an on-time God. Yes, he is! We made care packages for the homeless and candy bags for the kids. It's a blessing to be in a position to be a blessing. Thank you, Lord. I am in a state of amazement not just because we have gifts under the tree now but the lesson that I learned which is God is my source, my provider, and my way maker. He's my miracle worker, and I need to be still and wait on him.

> Take delight in the lord, and he will give you the desires of your heart. (Psalm 37:4, NIV)

Chapter 6

False Prophets

Beware of false prophets, which come to you in sheep's
clothing, but inwardly they are raving wolves.
　　　　　　　　　　　　　　　　　—Matthew 7:15

Happy New Year, it is Jan 1, 2016. Glory be to God. He
saw fit to keep me another year. God has a mission for my
life, one which I am extremely aware of now more than ever.
I haven't been able to write anything since the Christmas
miracle of 2015. It's been almost a week that God has not
been leading me to write anything. Don't get me wrong.
I've gone to the library twice, but God was silent.

　　I began thinking like, *Lord, is that all we're going to talk
about?* I have an outline with a few more topics we haven't
even touched on yet. Testimony Tammy has a lot more testimony to tell. I decided not to be anxious and applied myself
to a deeper study in his Word and prayer. Nevertheless, God
had a little detour in mind at the same time.

> And he said unto them, "This kind
> can come forth by nothing, but by prayer
> and fasting. (Mark 9:29)

Studying, seeking revelations, committed fasting, and praying with the Holy Spirit leading had to take place in me before this half of the book was written. Immediately I allowed the Comforter to lead me and guide me to study in the Old Testament, revealing to me just how much God really does love each and every one of his children, how God wants us all to consistently pursue wholeness in our lives.

He revealed some things that had to get crucified in me, aspects of me that sat dormant until situations surfaced, as well as some things I intentionally overlooked in people close to me. Furthermore, before the blessing of this book could be released, there were some things I had to do and see. These types of things can only come from exposure, prayer, fasting, and the Word.

> Study to shew thyself approved unto God, a workman that needth not be ashamed, rightly dividing the word of truth. (2 Timothy 2:15, KJV)

This year, on New Year's Eve, I planned to bring in my New Year in the Lord's house, giving him all the glory for having a purpose for me in the next year, as well as thanking him for being with me this last year. Last Sunday, my pastor announced that if you are unemployed, you need to be in his Monday Bible class. I'm thinking to myself like, *Okay, Lord, that's me. I'll be there,* seeing as though I am currently the queen of unemployment.

I did not realize what a blessing it is to be so close to seasoned wisdom, a wisdom that was genuinely and joyfully given to me was a privilege. In contrast, within my first Monday class, I gained a greater love, appreciation, and respect for my shepherd. This man of God is a true vessel being used by God, one that I genuinely respect and love.

This New Year's Eve, we had big plans. At Bible study, he explained how he wanted the watch service to go this year. God was leading him to have the congregation individually get up and give an account for their personal progress in Christ during 2015. This was a small-in-number church yet grand in the anointing.

Furthermore, this charged me to examine what exactly did God grow me up in. Also I was not comfortable talking in front of people at this time which instantly got me asking God in my head like, *You want me to reveal Testimony Tammy*, which is extremely scary to me. I still dread having presentations at school, knowing my last name Cotton, so I'm bound to be first every time.

No matter how much I study and research myself to death, soon as I have to get in front of the class, I get nervous, saying unlimited um's and sweating like a racehorse. It's so embarrassing. Nevertheless, this presentation was for God, so I was going to have to humble myself and do it.

> For it is not ye that speak, but the Spirit of your Father which speaketh in you (Matthew 10:20).

This scripture gave me the courage to be able to say, "Okay, Lord, I know lately I been feeling a little sprinkling on my lips every now and then. I believe you'll give me the words to say exactly when you want me to say them."

Anyway, we planned to have a good watch service and a potluck dinner. I purchased a giant salad ready to toss it up for the saints. We are going be healthy and whole in 2016. God has stuff for us to do.

Furthermore, I continued with my New Year's duties, my daughter and I were at the Laundromat when I got this blast call from the church saying our pastor is in the hospital. We need to go into corporate prayer. Instantly at the folding table, my daughter and I went into prayer for our shepherd. "We are a church where everyone is family." I'd heard my pastor say that line to every new member when they came up to join the church. I heard him say it to me three times, and I believed it every time. They welcomed me back as a family member that never left.

> For whosoever shall do the will of my father which is in heaven, the same is my brother, and sister, and mother. (Matthew 12:50)

Yes, I joined church, then joined again and rejoined until I got serious. I'll never forget meeting them in the county jail. It was nothing but my Lord and Savior that kept drawing me back to this church. I felt the word of God come forth with such power and anointing.

Our shepherd preached once a month. Then every week, it's a different elder or reverend giving the word straight from the Lord. I can only imagine what measures of consecration the Lord and pastor put them through in order to deliver the Word of God. Yet I know for a fact every time, it's a direct message from our God, one that I don't have to filter out the motives behind the message.

Besides pastor, every elder, and reverend encourage you to stay in your word before anything and back up everything with the word. God knew this was the foundation I needed, this priceless gift that God has given me through their tireless labor I will forever be grateful for.

Anyway, once we arrived home with the laundry and realized our plans were canceled, my daughter wanted me to drop her off for the weekend on the west side. I agreed and began to make some calls and see if I could visit one of my friends' watch service at their church (the wrong move!). I did it anyway though.

Now I visited this church before, but it has been a while. I vaguely remembered how they operate. It all came back to me once I arrived though. I normally overlook when people start running around the church or people passing out. It's not my place to judge, and everyone responds differently to a word—for example, I'm a for-sure crybaby when it comes to the word. Nevertheless, what I can't overlook is when the congregation screaming so loud during the sermon. I often wonder if anyone heard the word of God.

> Let all things be done decently and in order. (1 Corinthians 14:40)

I really did just intend on being in the house of the Lord when the New Year came in. At the beginning, I believed my motives were right. Consequently God had revealed His intentions for my traditions. I believe God used this as a teaching moment that I will never forget. I learned about just how much God really loves us. Even though our own traditions and decisions, he still loves us. When we have an inkling that this might not be right and we do it anyway, he still loves us and teaches us through it.

> For God so loved the world that he gave his only begotten Son, that whosoever believeth in him should not perish but have everlasting life. (John 3:16)

Although I try my hardest to be quiet and inconspicuous when I am in new places, somehow I always get singled out everywhere I go. It never fails. I know it is nothing short of the Holy Spirit living on the inside of me. Anyway after a difficult beginning and countless distractions, I received the word for 2016. The word was "this will be the year of unfolding blessings. God wants a yes from us. And everyone is getting a new house, so pack up all that you can carry."

The pastor also prophesied straight from the pulpit to a few individuals in the congregation about jobs and wealth. Everyone was so excited and encouraged, the praises went up. As for me, it sounded great. That's exactly what a sister needed to hear.

I don't know about everyone else, but I'm believing God for a new house in 2016. Now what I'm not sure about is if the word came straight from our God or straight from the pastors ipad.

> For they loved the praise of men more than the praise of God. (John 12:43)

What really made me think I had to get out of there quick is when the pastor gave all the lady pastors in the audience holy oil to come around and lay hands on the congregation. Soon as they got that holy oil, it felt like my forehead was the target. I was so nervous, I started shaking their hands and raising my arms like an infant trying to play patty-cake. I had never experienced anything like that.

> Lay hands suddenly on no man, neither be partaker of other men's sins: keep thyself pure. (1 Timothy 5:22)

Glory be to God. It ended about 10:30. I had no idea that the watch service didn't actually watch for the New Year to come in. This new year, I was learning some new life lessons. Once I left, I checked my phone, and I missed a call from my other friend whom I had reached out to when I was in search of a church to bring in the New Year at. She had texted me the address of her watch service.

I was thinking, *Hey, I was still on the west side, and it's not actually midnight yet* (wrong move again). I should have gone home and been in my Word and on my knees, praying to God at midnight. Yet here I am chasing the sanctuary, completely ignoring the fact that I am the church.

> Don't you know that you are God's temple and that God's Spirit dwells in your midst? (1 Corinthians 3:16)

This experience has made me even more grateful to God for his patience and mercy. I often tell myself when I go have a manicure or a pedicure that I have to "go where

I know." That's just a little saying I use to keep me from wasting time or being disappointed with the results—just because they are Chinese don't mean they know how to do nails—which is a principle I should have stuck to on this New Year's Eve.

> Follow justice and justice alone, so that you may live and possess the land the Lord your God is giving you. (Deuteronomy 16:20)

Nevertheless, against my better judgment, I pulled up to my second friend's watch service. I couldn't find it at first. I looked right past the building. It was a place I had been to before for a basketball game. Once I went inside, yes, this gymnasium/sanctuary/restaurant/community center was the place. After I found my friend, I have no idea what I witnessed next.

I painfully listened to four different pastors scream, holler, sweat, and spit. I don't have any idea what either one of them said (seriously). It was more animated than anointed. My heart broke for the congregation. I began to pray for the members so heavily. It was definitely prompted by God.

> And he taught, saying unto them, Is it not written," My house shall be called of all nations the house of prayer? but ye have made it a den of thieves." (Mark 11:17)

Of course, I had to be sitting next to the speaker, and the echo of the gym made it impossible to hear. By now, I realized the Lord was silently punishing me for my traditions, so I just endured. I gave up on hearing the word altogether, yet if others still had hope, The organ boy was going to kill that. He stole any glory God was entitled. He was doing so much gyrating that I believe an elder organ player came and politely scooted him off the bench. However, he was not done yet. He surprisingly proceeded to the drums. I was in complete and utter shock. Over there, he beat those sticks harder than the boys with buckets do on the side of the Chicago expressway begging for change.

> But thou, O man of God, Flee these things; and follow after righteousness, godliness, faith, love, patience, meekness. (1 Timothy 6:11)

Chapter 7

Drugs

He that over cometh shall inherit all things; and
I will be his God, and he shall be my son.
—Revelation 21:7

Drugs and alcohol have always been a part of my life since I moved to the housing projects. I can remember the first time I ever smoked marijuana or took a sip of alcohol. I couldn't have been more than fourteen years old.

When I first started smoking, I was trying to hang with the cool kids. When you move around a lot, you become the new kid over and over again. It becomes difficult to adjust, so you want to try to fit in. Just imagine being the new kid every school year. It can be scary sometimes, especially if you have no foundation and don't know who you are.

> For no other foundation can anyone lay than that is laid, which is Jesus Christ. (1 Corinthians 3:11)

Every group home, jailhouse day room, strip club, dressing room, and party scene glorified the lifestyle of drugs and alcohol. No matter if it was bought, grown, or prescribed, my environments welcomed it as normal. Of course, I joined in thinking I would be perceived as abnormal if I didn't participate. When I was young, I even tried cigarettes but couldn't get hooked. The weed smoking only stuck with me because everywhere I went, they did it.

I hated the effects of the weed because it would always make me sleepy, quiet, or hungry which are character traits I don't like. Being sleepy I would be missing my money. Being quiet is definitely not me, and always eating wouldn't get me in my skinny jeans. This type of high had to be mixed with something that could bring me life (as I used to call it). That something was alcohol, although alcohol is a central-nervous-system depressant. This addictive combo sure puts a smile on my face.

Before I started drinking alcohol heavy, I would abuse energy drinks and coffee like crazy, thinking if I had more energy, somehow I'd magically add a few extra hours to my God given 24. I used to pride myself on how much stuff I could get established in a day. Normally I would accomplish a number of tasks before and after work. That's why weed was definitely not my drug of choice. It was my drug of influence and lifestyle.

Although I didn't like the effects of smoking weed, I did it every day. After doing it every day for a while, I would long for it, having attitudes when I couldn't get high as soon as I wanted to. Even when I was working good jobs as a tax collector and office manager, I was still getting high as a kite. Soon as I left the office, I was racing to get high, sometimes even getting high before I went into work. I recall a time when I'd get high before I went to church. This is so sad but so true.

> Jesus said, "Father, forgive them, for they do not know what they are doing." And they divided up his clothes by casting lots. (Luke 23:34)

Smoking weed, drinking alcohol, partying, and sex definitely come with the lifestyle of a hustler, no matter if you are selling clothes, drugs, playing cards, or selling your body, whatever your scam is. Once you and your fellow hustlers get a good scam, it is time to celebrate. The drugs and alcohol were not far behind, and neither was county jail.

Now after an exhausting lifestyle of partying and going in and out of jail, a few judges would mandate me to do drug treatment which I took with the quickness, thinking it was a "get out of jail free" card in the monopoly game of my life. While in these classes, I listened and realized their literature and guidance was substantial for a recovering addict that really wanted to recover. If they applied them twelve steps, I believed in my heart, complete restoration was attainable.

I remember their step number one was "we admitted we were powerless over our addiction that our lives have become unmanageable." Notice how I said *their* step number one.

Back then, as I sat in those mandatory meetings, just cooperating in order to stay free, nobody could convince me that I had an addiction. I would say things like "Their story was nothing like mine," "I'm not a crackhead," "They do anything for a hit," "It's only smoking weed," and, "Alcohol is legal."

> Thou hypocrite, first cast out the beam out of thine own eye; and then shalt thou see clearly to cast out the mote out of thy brother's eye. (Matthew 7:5)

Society, social media, and my environment told me this is normal. How can they tell me to admit that my life has become unmanageable? I managed to make this meeting and not go back to jail, so I was better than step number one, or so I thought.

Certainly, now that I've surrendered my will unto God's will for my life, I see clearly that I had one of the worst addictions an addict could have, an addiction that's so deep-rooted that the addict is oblivious to the fact that they are even an addict. Now, that is the worst kind of addiction. I was not only addicted to the drugs and alcohol but to the whole lifestyle. I am more than grateful for my numerous incarcerations now more than ever. God loved me so much, he saved me from myself, using my incarceration as an opportunity to seek God's face.

> Therefore, behold, I will allure her, and bring her into the wilderness, and speak comfortably unto her. (Hosea 2:14)

Over ten years of partying every night, popping bottles, and shopping every day, trying to dress up a mess, it began to take a toll on my body and my energy. I started to stay in and miss all kinds of money. I would become exhausted quickly, and there was nothing worse than a lazy stripper or an online prostitute. I was slowly losing my edge in the money game. The name of the hustle game is Endurance—if you could dance and look good all night, every night, also be quick and clever to the tricks you were winning as a stripper and online.

> For what is a man profited, if he shall gain the whole world, and lose his own soul? or what shall a man give in exchange for his soul? (Matthew 16:26)

This was around the time I was introduced to the ecstasy pill. This drug was definitely my drug of choice. It made me think I was invincible in every aspect. Once I popped my first pill, I was so high. I could not stop moving. Ecstasy had me believing that I was more focused than normal, that I was quicker and clever with my responses to people. In the beginning, I could get so much of my business done and still party all night.

I started popping pills every day, sometimes twice a day. Undoubtedly I had to have one every time I stepped foot on the party scene, hunting down the darker pills, thinking they were the ones with the most drugs on them. In turn, I would be even higher if I find that kind. Anticipating the moment of nausea hitting my stomach, indicating "go to the bathroom," I happily went to vomit or diarrhea which means I am about to be extremely high. I thought ecstasy made me feel so good. Once I was high, I could perform every ungodly act with my ecstasy mask called "a smile."

> Whoredom and wine and new wine take away the heart. (Hosea 4:11)

After studying this drug in school, I learned that psychologically ecstasy makes you think you are functioning at the best of your ability when in reality, you are not even close. Sometimes I would be moving so fast I could not keep up with myself. In the club, I was the life of the party.

Yet in professional settings, I would chew gum to hide grinding my teeth, drink unlimited water so no one would notice the white forming in the cracks of my mouth from dehydration. My heart would be racing as I stayed up for days at a time, never allowing myself to go to sleep.

After using the drug for an extended period of time, what the drug dealers and your fellow party goers don't tell you is the long-term effects, like long-term confusion, sleeplessness, depression, fatigue, lack of motivation and drive and lack of empathy. I used to struggle with all of these after effects until I gave my life to God completely.

> Therefore if any man be in Christ, he is a new creature: old things are passed away; behold, all things are become new. (2 Corinthians 5:17)

In the twelve steps to recovery, step number says, "Came to believe a Power greater than our selves could restore us back to sanity." I truly believe the twelve steps are God-breathed; and once you get to step number two, you are cooking with gas now. Once you believe the Holy Spirit steps in to help guide you to glory. Then in step number three, "Made a decision to turn our will and our lives over to the care of God as we understood God." You on fire with this step, and all the other steps fall in order. I believe in the power of God and the process of recovery. I believe so much that I'm now a certified alcohol-and-drug counselor. I have the privilege to counsel people through some of the same issues God counseled me through.

> Being confident of this very thing, that which hath began a good work in you will perform it until the day of Jesus Christ. (Philippians 1:6)

Chapter 8

Jail

If the Son therefore shall make you
free, ye shall be free indeed.
—John 8:36 (KJV)

Being locked up is definitely apart of who I am. I have been to the county jail so many times I have lost count, not to mention other county jails and two different penitentiaries which means I have a little experience in this area. Seems like every hustle I ever did, I definitely suffered the consequences for it. Even traffic violations, I went to jail for them as well.

The county jail became my second home. I was there so often that as soon as I came in, I would get a job in the hallways. Having a job in the hallways is a big thing in jail. You come out of your unit every day to clean the hallways, wash uniforms, or prepare food. Having a job in jail, you look forward to having something productive to do. It also makes your sentence appear to go by faster—definitely beats watching TV, playing cards in the day room, and gossiping about the inmate couples all day—anticipating the next fight just to have some sort of live entertainment, basically just watching the clock as life passes you by.

You become so consumed with working in the hallways that by the time you are done, you can mark that day off on your calendar. Like some people in this world today, they become so busy that time just flies by. Then before you know it, it's time to stand before the judge, our Lord and Creator.

> And the cares of this world, and the deceitfulness of riches, and lust of other things entering in, choke out the word, and it becometh unfruitful. (Mark 4:19, KJV)

A few perks of working in the jailhouse hallways, besides the fact that it was time-consuming, is you get new uniforms daily, a bit of notoriety amongst the inmates, and a real meal from the officers every now and then, which is great, considering the mystery meals that would be on the trays at dinner time. No matter how much commissary snacks an inmate buys, it's only so many dips, burritos, and nachos a person can handle before it's not even exciting anymore. Sort of like the real world, even living in abundance, you can still feel desolate.

Nevertheless, it's interesting to see how commissary day brings out the arrogance and selfishness in an inmate. Women would literally come in dope sick and in high pursuit of something sweet to eat. Yet the moment their lover or grandma sends them some money, they go from begging for a piece of candy to arrogantly refusing to give the next person anything.

> I have shewed you all things, how that so laboring ye ought to support the weak, and to remember the words of the Lord Jesus how he said, it is more blessed to give than to receive. (Acts 20:35, KJV)

As well as the young girls who come to jail, claiming to be billion-dollar bosses. It's a heartbreaking epidemic in teens today. Name brands, fast money, drugs, and alcohol are glorified in the streets of Chicago. It also happens in jail. A person is defined by how many bags they come from commissary with, although some of the people with unlimited bags from commissary might be the same ones smoking bags in the streets.

> Let no man therefore judge you in meat, or in drink, or in respect of an holy-day, or of the new moon, or of the sabbath days. (Colossians 2:16, KJV)

It never amazes me with some of the lengths women in jail would go to when they know they won't make it to shop commissary. Some would purposely pick fights just to go to the hole, knowing the consequence is a restriction from shopping commissary. Yet all along, they had no funds available, instead of staying in population and eating what the state provides. It's hard to handle watching someone else indulge in the commissary, something like the world today where some can't handle watching someone else profit. Pride would make them go to great measures if they can't have what the next person has.

> When pride cometh, then cometh shame: but with the lowly is wisdom. (Proverbs 11:2, KJV)

Some of the people who did shop commissary every week, you could tell who they were. Those were the ones that got bigger and bigger as the days went by, eating some of what the state provided, then going back in their cells and creating a feast, not to mention candy bars, honey buns, cupcakes, and cookies. The lack of self-discipline would allow some to use food as a crutch during their jail time.

> But godliness and contentment is great gain. (1 Timothy 6:6, KJV)

When a person is in jail, people sit and watch your demeanor, how many calls you get through to the world, or if you get visits. This determines to the onlookers whether they'll even talk to you or not, let alone help you. If it seems like you might get some assistance from the world, then they might give you an old deodorant or candy bar, nevertheless with the expectation of asking for that favor back later. There is no charity in jail, only the *barter system* which is if I give you something now, then you owe me something later, something similar to the world today, just replacing the cash with commissary.

Next, let me say this to the cash-collecting-corrections system. "Rehabilitation is a state of mind!" Locking a person up for an unlimited amount of months or years will not change the way they think. To change a person's behavior, they must first change the way they think about their behavior. That is why the corrections system was a revolving door for me and most. There is no correcting in the county jail, only convictions.

As a matter of fact, the inmates' thinking become so distorted during the time of incarceration. Some would begin to think of ways they could do the same crime differently, creatively and carefully using the time to plan new hustles. Inmate's creativity becomes limitless when they are limited. Besides creating new strategies for crimes, women inmates create tampons, mops, head scarfs, makeup, clothes, weapons. You name it. They have created it.

Some even create a superficial high, using the nurses as prescription drug dealers, creating all these injuries just to get a prescription for pain, trying to either sleep their time away or using the "barter system" on commissary day, once again, something just like this earthly world. Some will use drugs and alcohol to relieve the pain. I know I did. Either way, in such a desolate situation, the thinking is still get high or hustle. We must first change the way we think. Change has to happen at the root of us, not the fruit of us.

> And be not conformed to this world: but be ye transformed by the renewing of your mind, that ye may prove what is that good, and acceptable, and perfect, will of God. (Romans 12:2, KJV)

Of course, I was a victim and willing participant in this type of thinking as well. Not once did I think during countless incarcerations that this lifestyle will not suffice until I surrendered myself to the plan and purpose that

God had for my life, daily putting on the helmet of salvation and the full armor of God. Now I can say without a doubt that my thinking is different.

Nevertheless, let me say this: everything that happened in the county was not all bad. Neither was every inmate just rotten to the core. Some of the officers were just one crime away from swapping uniforms with me. Furthermore, while I was in the county jail, I obtained my GED certificate which I know at that time in my life, if I was not in jail, I would have never achieved. Also, I'm so proud to say that my time in jail helped me to realize God's presence is a privilege. If we are not careful, the distractions of this world will rob us of quiet time with God.

Therefore I want to put to bed the notion when people say, "Inmates go to jail and find God." Or they say, "We come out all spiritual." Let me be clear. God was with me before I went to jail. His grace and mercy rescued me from myself. As you can see in this chapter, there are plenty of distractions even in jail. I went to jail on numerous occasions and did not find God, although he was definitely there. We don't have to answer the call. We're just provided to an opportunity with minimum distractions. I believe every inmate in the system has a purpose for their pain.

For many are called but few are chosen. (Matthew 22:14, KJV)

Now before I begin to get serious with God, I watched numerous churches come into the jail and preach the gospel. I remember listening but never really paying attention unless it was a church that demanded respect. I would go, just to get off the unit, or to see if they had any care packages. Of course, I didn't want to miss out on some real soap or sox's or something.

I remember when I first met the church that planted the desire in me to study God's word. I was crying like a baby because the presence of God was so heavy. My mentor came in with such seriousness and authority. The boldness of her faith was so appealing to me. I remember telling the little bitty lady to give me their information, I'm coming home Friday, and I was coming to their church Sunday. That is exactly what I did, although I didn't get it right off the back. I thank God for not allowing me to have any shame because I joined and joined and rejoined until I got it. In between me joining and rejoining, there were a few more incarcerations and imprisonments.

My last prison sentence was the longest and most life-changing. Prison is much different from county jail. It's like another type of air you breathe. If you are not grounded, prison can choke the hope right out of you. I remember the clouds were even shaped different and thicker. The water had a rusty old unique aftertaste, even the inmates had a humble and content mind-set no matter how much time they had. There were women sentenced to life that would be so cheerful every day, knowing that their expected end was a wooden box over in the inmate cemetery.

When I first arrived in the prison, they put me in a cell for days until I was medically clear to go into the population. They gave me toiletries, and my choice of a Bible or a book. This time, I chose the Bible only because it had a lot of books in one, not knowing these books would transform my mind. I recall staying up all night and day reading the book of Matthew and crying as if I was there. I felt the pain of Jesus so vividly. I had never read a book before that made me cry. Things got so intense for me, I had to open the window for some fresh air. I began talking to God that day and came to a understanding.

For God so loved the world, that he gave his only begotten Son, that whosoever believeth in him should not perish, but have everlasting life (John 3:16, KJV).

Chapter 9

Lesbianism

> For this cause God gave them up unto vile affections: for even their own women did change the natural use into that which is against nature.
> —Romans 1:26 (KJV)

The devil is patient and strategic in getting his business done. As I stated in previous chapters, Satan plants seeds, then patiently awaits a harvest which is exactly what he did in this area of my life called lesbianism. Having me raped, continuously molested, and lesbian chat lines—these were all seeds of bondage periodically planted by the devil.

> For we wrestle not against flesh and blood, but against principalities, against powers, against the rulers of the darkness of this world, against spiritual wickedness in high places. (Ephesians 6:12, KJV)

I believe it was my second time going to prison. I was pregnant with my second daughter named Ianna which means God is gracious. I often tell her that her name says it all because God's grace is the reason she is here today. Seeing as though I had three abortions before delivering her, God's grace and her purpose locked me up in prison to deliver her.

Now when you are pregnant in prison, they put all the pregnant girls in the drug treatment unit. Being pregnant and in prison is one meltdown waiting to happen. Then being on a unit full of pregnant girls and recovering alcohol or drug addicts, that's another level of pain you can't even imagine. There was a different meltdown every day. Some say prison is the devil's playground.

I was emotional, uncertain, lonely, worried, and sentenced to three years, fertile ground for the devil to reap the harvest of his many seeds previously planted in my mind.

Normally when I go to the county jail, I bond out. Or my lawyer finds a glitch, and I catch a miracle. Prison, on the other hand, is another story. Reality sets in that your freedom is gone. There's no more hoping every court date that you might catch a blessing. You're there until your time is up, a definite wilderness for a woman that's pregnant and uncertain of who she is in Christ.

Then this beautiful lesbian girl comes out of the clear blue, showing me all this attention and wanting to help with everything that I needed, concerned with everything that concerns me, listening to every complaint that comes out of my mouth, making me feel loved and wanted at a time in my life when I had no idea how much God loves and wants me.

> They are the kind who worm their way into homes and gain control over gullible women, who are loaded down with sin and are swayed by all kinds of evil desires. (2 Timothy 3:6, NIV)

In the beginning, this girl stuck to me like glue, which was kind of normal in prison only because even if you are not a lesbian, there are these silent cliques. Mexicans hang with the Mexicans, whites with whites, lesbians with lesbians, even Christians with Christians. A girlfriend, on the other hand, is a little more intense.

We began to comfort each other during our time of vulnerability. We were separated once the officers found out we were a couple. Then we began chasing each other around the prison grounds, anticipating our next romantic encounter, sneaking in hugs and kisses every time we got a chance. We would write love letters, sharing our thoughts and similarities. I started to think about her all the time, allowing lust to consume my mind.

> Casting down imaginations, and every high thing that exalteth itself against the knowledge of God, and bringing into captivity every thought to the obedience of Christ. (2 Corinthians 10:5, KJV)

Nevertheless, this lesbian knew the Lord. She would quote scriptures and everything. I remember we would meet each other in the church sometimes. Furthermore, no matter how good the choir was or how enlightening and aggressive the preacher was, she would say or do something to distract me from the message, seemed like she would purposely gain my attention if I appeared too interested.

Now I should have left that spirit in prison, but we decided to continue this in the free world, one of my greatest mistakes! This girl was the worst of every girlfriend I ever had. We went through so many self-inflicted problems. It was abnormal. There was so many, I can't even count them all. I know once we became free, I noticed she was a lazy person, not wanting to work and nervous to hustle.

This didn't sit well with me. I have never been the type to financially support my mate. She would rather superficially help me with whatever hustle I was doing. That way, she would make me feel entitled to compensate her, although it seemed as if everything I allowed her to be involved with would crumble.

I recall she was the one who brought me numerous girls for my online prostitution hustle. The same girls she brought me was the same girls that got my face plastered all over the news as one of the first girls to get caught holding a house of prostitution and pimping online. That was the most embarrassing thing that ever happened to me, although I did numerous degrading things at that point. The exposure brought the shame.

> For I acknowledge my transgressions: and my sin is ever before me. (Psalm 51:3, KJV)

Of course, I dated many other girls after her, countless dysfunctional lesbian relationships, not even aware that if God can't get the glory in it, then it will never prosper. No matter how loving the lesbian relationship appeared, it's nothing but lust. Only God knows exactly what is really going on when the curtains close.

Nevertheless, let me fast forward to the last lesbian relationship I had. She was very young and hopelessness toward her own future. I mean seriously, she loved to party and do drugs. That was the extent of her life's ambitions. My youngest daughter and I moved in with her and her mother after a few months. Her mother was a very old Christian lady who was extremely sweet, but it seemed as if she was worn out from all the drama her kids have put her through.

At this time, I was still stripping and partying every night. She would watch my daughter and take her to school also. I stayed because of some sort of drug class to maintain my freedom. After I moved in, she began to get on my nerves. I saved my dancing money and got my own apartment. Then I broke up with her, and she did not like that at all. She stayed, calling and texting, trying to work it out. Although my mind said this is over, my flesh longed for the affection it was used too which made me give in to her and let her come over to my new place.

> Therefore God gave them over to the sinful desires of their hearts to sexual impurity for the degrading of their bodies with one another. (Romans 1:24, NIV)

After making up with each other the whole day, that same night, I had a few private stripper parties to do. Also, my old friends from the projects were having some sort of reunion party. I decided to take her with me to do my shows. That way, when I was done, we could go straight to the reunion. We began to get dressed and go pick up my pills, weed, and liquor, all the things I needed in order to submit myself to the will of these men.

I made a little money at the first show. Then in the second show, that's where I made a good amount. While in the dressing room, we decided to pop our pills now because it's time to go party. After gathering all my money together, it was so fat that I could not put it in my bra. Mind you, I had on this tiny leopard dress, and she had on some cargo pants. Therefore, it made more sense to put all my money in her pocket, or so I thought.

> Trust in the Lord with all thine heart; and lean not unto thine own understanding. (Proverbs 3:5, KJV)

Now we in the streets, riding, drinking, and smoking, on our way to go party with my project friends who she never met before. When we pulled up, we sat outside to finish our cups of liquor which gave me a chance to put my hills back on. I always take them off when I'm driving. Meanwhile, we are high as kites off ecstasy pills, mingled it with weed and liquor.

Once we walked into the project party, it was over. Everyone was leaving. Yet two of my friends wanted to hop in with me to find an after-hour's club. They didn't have any money. But I said, "Come on, I'll pay." I really wanted to continue partying. She gave me a little smirk, but I overlooked it at the time.

Thereafter we pulled up to the club, and my girlfriend had to put her knife in the glove compartment or else she could not get in. Consequently all of us could not get in any way because one of my friends didn't have her ID. We kept it moving to drop her off with her boyfriend. That way, my girl, my buddy, Mya, and me could still go partying. Normally when I'm high on pills, I'm in a rush, so she was slowing our party down.

Finally we're on our way to the party, and we stopped at the gas station on Halsted Street. She went in to get some blunts. And Mya got to telling me that my girlfriend was tripping about me paying for everybody, and I was not paying attention. I was shocked because I was so high off the drugs, I didn't even acknowledge her attitude. In addition, I'm shocked because she's tripping about how I want to spend my own money.

> A wise man will hear, and will increase learning; and a man of understanding shall attain unto wise counselors. (Proverbs 1:5, KJV)

Certainly, once she got back into the car, I began to listen to her. She was casually talking slick saying things like I'm doing too much and spending too much money. Next, I turned the music down and told her, "I don't care what you are talking about. Just give me my money out of your pocket."

She replied, "Just wait until later once we get home."

"No, I will take you home right now."

Remember it's about 4:00 a.m.; and we still drinking, driving, smoking and all with no driver's license. I was so high, I did not care, still speeding so fast that Mya was in the back seat scared for her life. I took my hand off the wheel, trying to reach over to grab my money out of her pocket, and she pushed me back. It then escalated to a rumble while I'm now speeding, coming down 63 Street. I made a right turn on Ashland where I saw the police truck pulled over in the middle of a traffic stop. Then something clear as day whispered in my ear and said, "Stop right here." I will never forget.

He that hath ears to hear, let him hear. (Matthew 11:15, KJV)

This voice made me pull right on the side of the officer truck. I rolled down her side window and talked to the officer right across her lap. I said, "Officer, can you please get her out of my car? She won't give me my money back."

He replied, "No, can't you see I'm in the middle of a traffic stop. Keep going down Ashland into the station."

Something made me say, "No, officer, I'll wait." So I reversed my car and parked right behind the officer truck. She started going crazy talking about how she has a warrant and I'm trying to send her to jail. She opened up the car door and stepped out as if she was about to run. Then she leaned back in and opened up the glove compartment, grabbed her knife, and started stabbing me multiple times.

I shifted my body and started kicking for my life. Since I didn't have any shoes on, the knife was cutting my feet a lot. As she charged at my face with the knife, I swung my arm over which made me received a deep stab right through the top of my arm and came out the bottom. She just began to go crazy and continue to slice my body.

For our light affliction, which is but for a moment, worketh for us a far more exceeding and eternal weight of glory. (2 Corinthians 4:17, KJV)

I began to use my right arm to reach behind me and open my door. I eased my body backward onto the ground. Now once she saw that I was out of the car, she got back into my car, proceeded to hop over to the driver side, and steal my car. All this happened as the police stood at the hood of my car watching.

Mya was still in the back seat. She hopped out of the car as it was in motion. She ran over to me as I crawled to the curb. Blood was everywhere as she held me in her arms. She kept saying, "Tammy you not gone die. Tammy, you not gone die. Tammy, you not gone die."

I remember saying, "I think I am."

> And Jesus saith unto him, I will come and heal him. (Matthew 8:7, KJV)

Once I arrived at the hospital, the doctors said I had two major stab wounds, seven severe cuts and numerous minor cuts on my legs and feet. It was a miracle that the knife didn't hit anything major. Yet they still had to stitch me up. Then they put a tube in my leg to drain any infections from the knife.

The nerve damage was so severe that I could not walk. I moved in with my friend and his girlfriend. They literally had to put a chair in the shower so that I could bathe. This was one of the hardest times of my life. I would get so frustrated using the crutches that I went into a deep depression.

After being miserable for months, it's like one day, I just snapped out of it. I asked my friend to take me to go buy me a cane, and I would force myself to get up and go places. My first painful trip was to the police headquarters. I wanted to press charges on the cops that watched this girl stab me. I endlessly went back and forth down to that station. Eventually they were found not guilty, and the case was closed. I could not believe it.

> It is mine to avenge; I will repay. In due time their foot will slip; their day of disaster is near and their doom rushes upon them. (Deuteronomy 32:35, NIV)

Chapter 10

The Process

> Knowing this, that the trying of your
> faith worketh patience.
>
> —James 1:3 (KJV)

This is the final chapter of this book. To God be the glory. The first nine chapters had unlimited intermissions between breakthroughs. However, this final chapter took about one year to complete, another year to revise, and another year for inner growth. Some say our God works in three's. I was definitely in the potter's house going through "the process," from God putting a twinkle in my eye and the devil having me think I had a bad eyelash installed to having countless visions and dreams that I know for a fact was God, a constant voice in my head saying, "I'm pregnant, I'm pregnant." Nevertheless, at this time, I was practicing abstinence. I completely disregarded the voice, oblivious to the fact that was God whispering to me that I'm pregnant with purpose.

During the first year of my unplanned sabbatical, I began to doubt if this is really what God told me to do. Every time I would try to complete this book, life would hit harder than normal, and I'd let the devil distract me. Nonetheless, when reality sat in, I know it was not my bright idea to write this book, nor was it my own self-discipline that sat me down to complete it. This commitment was definitely God. I came to realize the sabbatical was a part of my molding process in the potter's house. Many aspects of me had to die before God could live within me.

During this journey, I lost every job except one. I was serving for upscale events. Now, isn't this ironic? I had to learn to serve. The last job that God allowed me to keep was every Saturday at this beautiful venue that held wedding receptions. This was a very high-class place, thousands of dollars just for the venue, not to mention the bartenders, caterers, planners, musicians, florist, and more. Let's just say if you booked a night, you had some real money.

Now with this being my only job, I would often go into prayer, asking God, "What do I need to learn in this environment?" Why is this my only job? Please enlighten me on what I might be overlooking or missing within myself.

Nevertheless, one day, the job sent us bartenders out to a new venue. This very fancy private art studio. I walked in, and it had pictures of all these famous people hanging up. As the wedding is going on, some older white man comes to the bar requesting a wine. Normally we can't pour drinks until the weddings over, but my boss said he's the owner of the art studio and the artist behind all the beautiful pieces. I'm guessing it is okay to pour him some wine. We began to talk about life. This man was filled with funny stories.

He made me feel as if he was really interested in my conversation. So I told him about this book I was writing and the vision I had for the cover, how much I really would appreciate his opinion seeing as though he is an award-winning artist. He began to stare at my face as if analyzing if for some purpose. After a long pause, he pours out the vision you see on the cover of this book. I asked him, "How much would it cost me?" He said I couldn't afford him. And boy, was he right. Then he said he will do it for free. To God be the glory.

> Give thanks to the Lord of lords: His love endures forever. (Psalm 136:3, NIV)

When I first got into the hospitality industry, I was getting hired at every catering and staffing company I signed up for. As a matter of fact, the hospitality industry was the only industry I could get into, never realizing Gods plan from the beginning because in hospitality, it's all about service, how to have an approachable demeanor. That way, people would feel comfortable with me serving them. God was working something out of me that couldn't go where he was taking me—for example, always serving people with a smile and catering to their needs with patience and meekness. At the beginning, serving others was very humbling, but now it's my passion.

Last year alone, I worked for six different companies just to gain full-time employment. I was laboring all over the place. I worked so much, I barely saw my daughters, thinking if I'm busy making money, then it's okay, not realizing we can be so busy making money to deposit it into a purse with holes.

> For we hear that there are some which walk among you disorderly, working not at all, but are busybodies. (Psalm 136:3, KJV)

That part of me had to go. I needed to gain some couth, education, skill, and more. Once God opened up my busy schedule (getting fired), money became really tight. I had to borrow money from the church to pay my rent which was a very humbling experience for me. This was before the Christmas miracle and the revelation about the chapter on miracles. I was oblivious to the fact that God was a very present help in my time of trouble, even then as he allowed the situation to happen in the first place, using my circumstances to build of my faith and my character. For a long time, I never knew that is what was going on. I believed God all the way up to a certain point. then couldn't press past the fear of what's on the other side. I just failed the test, then consequently took the same test over and over again. Finally, I realized the lesson to be learned was bigger than my little rent being due or money being low. This epiphany surged me to study the area of God's word where it says,

> Therefore I take pleasure in infirmities, in reproaches, in necessities, in persecutions, in distresses for Christ's sake: for when I am weak, then am I strong. (2 Corinthians 12:10, KJV)

I believed this scripture so much I was determined to smile when hardships arrive. Then one of my favorite authors came out with a book about happiness. I was the first to purchase it, thinking God was right on time with this one. As a result, a different level of warfare came upon me like I never experienced before. This book had the opposite effect. I was depressed on a whole new level.

Just a sad case of sadness, it was pathetic. I became so lazy to the point I couldn't even get out of bed, and worried to the point that I couldn't shake it off, if I had a map to my miracle. I had never experienced anything like it before.

The worst part about it was I was currently in a weekly Bible study on spiritual warfare. Knowing that was a trick of the enemy, I couldn't shake that depression for anything. This part of my process was truly a teaching moment. I learned to push through no matter what I felt like. That depression was a doorway for the devil to have a field day with my feelings and my faith. I started to realize the devil won't stop, so I have to choose to be happy every day, committing myself to daily walk in the joy of the Lord.

Once rent time rolled around again, I was back in a circle of testing again. I was determined to pass the test this time. I was going to talk to the landlord or something, but what I was not going to do was backslide into stripping or using men for money. I am delivered from that, and there is no turning back. No matter what the situation looks like, I have to stand on what I know about God.

> Cast your cares on the Lord, and he shall sustain you; he will never let the righteous be shaken (Psalm 55:22, NIV).

I have been delivered from lesbianism, hopelessness, anger, unforgiveness, drugs and alcohol, prostitution, street hustling, and countless other bondages. I know the devil tries to bring us back into bondage, but we have to stand still in our breakthroughs, knowing this too shall pass.

Nevertheless, some areas of our warfare are stronger than the others. The devil has mastered his craft. We as Christians have to master casting down the thoughts that we know are not of God. The difference now is none shall take root, and none shall blossom in the mighty name of Jesus. I put on the helmet of salvation daily that I may stand against the devil. He will not stop his attacks; but he will know that messing with this child of God, I have the victory.

I've been on countless interviews and never got the job. Even interviews that I was overqualified for, I'd get the door slammed in my face. Sometimes I would wonder, *What's going on, Lord?* Then I learned to get quiet and use the time to draw closer to God. He guided me to go back to college, something that I never even thought about. Now I have my degree in addiction studies and working in a treatment facility where I have the privilege of helping others in bondage to achieve breakthroughs. I am also studying for my master's degree, which is an amazing feeling. To God be the Glory. Lord willing, I plan to open up my own recovery home to help ex-offenders gain the tools they need to never go back to jail, a recovery home that has a foundation built on the word of God, ran with integrity and wisdom, encouraging sisters to,

Seek first his kingdom and his righteousness, and all these things will be given to you as well (Matthew 6:33, NIV).

Also during this season, he ordered my steps to join the street evangelism ministry. Here, I gained a heart for the lost souls and a desire to enlighten them about the goodness of God. The street witnessing team was not an accident. This season was ordained by God to transform my heart into a genuine heart of compassion for his people.

During this part of my process, I gained the most revelation about God's love and mercy than I'd ever known before. I began to fall in love with who God truly is. His desires and plans became my desires and plans. I witnessed people cry out to God and fall into my arms for comfort, watching evil spirits be cast down, as well as total strangers giving their life to Christ. God has a call on my life and yours. I pray right now that you answer.

> "For I know the plans I have for you," declares the Lord "plans to prosper you and not to harm you, plans to give you hope and a future." (Jeremiah 29:11, NIV)

The last thing I learned during this process is some people are only in our lives for a season. God does not want us to build a house where we should have pitched a tent. Furthermore, God will always have new ideas and plans as well as methods of executing them. This allows us the opportunity to always depend on God's will for our lives which is far better than we can ever imagine.

> As the heavens are higher than the earth, so are my ways higher than your ways, and my thoughts than your thoughts. (Isaiah 55:9, NIV)

Let's Socialize

What has been will be again, what has been done will
be done again; there is nothing new under the sun.
—Isaiah 55:9

This scripture came to me with the idea of "Lets Socialize."
I know for a fact that God sat me down to write this book
because my story is nothing new under the sun. I believe
if you are reading this book, some area of my story is your
story. God has a scripture for you that will enlighten and
encourage you. I want to know which one. I want to hear
from you.

So let's socialize. Take out your phone and follow me
on Facebook, Instagram or Twitter, @testimonytammy.
Then look to the table of contents to see which chapter
you think you are going to relate to and tag me in it. Then
after reading the book, which part of my story is your story,
which chapter you related to that you thought you were
the only one? Which scripture enlightened and encouraged
you? I'm excited to hear from you.

If God has been with me this whole time, he is with
you as well. No matter what you did or currently doing,
God still loves you. He also has a plan for your life just like
he had this planned for mine. I can't wait to hear from you.
May God bless you.

Acknowledgments

I have to give honor to God, my Savior, who's hand is throughout this book and written all over my life. I am in a continuous state of amazement when it comes to your character. You have loved me on a level that is unexplainable. This life-changing experience has been nothing short of agape love. I am grateful, and I could never repay you. Yet I will forever aim to please you.

The process to be continued.

About the Author

Tamera Cotton's life is the example of God's grace and mercy. She has overcome multiple bondages and achieved breakthroughs. Tamera currently works with women's recovery and reentry services. She currently holds an associate degree in addiction studies, a bachelor's degree in communication, and is pursuing a master's degree in social work. Tamera is an influential motivational speaker and philanthropist. She's also a single mother of two beautiful girls. Tamera strives to be an example of a Christian woman who consistently operates in integrity with the grace of God.

CPSIA information can be obtained
at www.ICGtesting.com
Printed in the USA
BVHW031554211019
561642BV00002BA/287/P

9 781645 696049